Why War?

First Warbler Classics Edition 2024

Why War? A Correspondence Between Albert Einstein and Sigmund Freud
first published by the International Institute of Intellectual Co-operation,
League of Nations, 1933

"Thoughts for the Times on War and Death" by Sigmund Freud first published
in *Imago* by Hugo Heller and Company, Vienna, 1915; first English translation in
Reflections on War and Death by Moffat, Yard, and Company, New York, 1918

ISBN 978-1-962572-17-0 (paperback)
ISBN 978-1-962572-18-7 (e-book)

warblerpress.com

Why War?

A CORRESPONDENCE
BETWEEN
ALBERT EINSTEIN
AND
SIGMUND FREUD

with additional writings

TRANSLATED BY STUART GILBERT

CONTENTS

WHY WAR?

ALBERT EINSTEIN

Caputh near Potsdam, 30th July, 1932.

Dear Professor Freud,

The proposal of the League of Nations and its International Institute of Intellectual Co-operation at Paris that I should invite a person, to be chosen by myself, to a frank exchange of views on any problem that I might select affords me a very welcome opportunity of conferring with you upon a question which, as things now are, seems the most insistent of all the problems civilisation has to face. This is the problem: Is there any way of delivering mankind from the menace of war? It is common knowledge that, with the advance of modern science, this issue has come to mean a matter of life and death for civilisation as we know it; nevertheless, for all the zeal displayed, every attempt at its solution has ended in a lamentable breakdown.

I believe, moreover, that those whose duty it is to tackle the problem professionally and practically are growing only too aware of their impotence to deal with it, and have now a very lively desire to learn the views of men who, absorbed in the pursuit of science, can see world-problems in the perspective distance lends. As for me, the normal objective of my thought affords no insight into the dark places of human will and feeling. Thus, in the enquiry now proposed, I can do little more than seek to clarify the question at issue and, clearing the ground of the more obvious solutions, enable you to bring the light of your far-reaching knowledge of man's instinctive life to bear upon the problem. There are certain psychological obstacles whose existence a layman in the mental sciences may dimly surmise, but whose interrelations and vagaries he is incompetent to fathom; you, I am convinced, will be able to suggest educative methods, lying more or less outside the scope of politics, which will eliminate these obstacles.

As one immune from nationalist bias, I personally see a simple way of dealing with the superficial (i.e. administrative) aspect of the problem: the setting up, by international consent, of a legislative and judicial body to settle every conflict arising between nations. Each nation would undertake to abide by the orders issued by this legislative body, to invoke its decision in every dispute, to accept its judgments unreservedly and to carry out every measure the tribunal deems necessary for the execution of its decrees. But here, at the outset, I come up against a difficulty; a tribunal is a human institution which, in proportion as the power at its disposal is inadequate to enforce its verdicts, is all the more prone to suffer these to be deflected by extrajudicial pressure. This is a fact with which we have to reckon; law and might inevitably go hand in hand, and juridical decisions approach more nearly the ideal justice demanded by the community (in whose name and interests these verdicts are pronounced) in so far as the community has effective power to compel respect of its juridical ideal. But at present we are far from possessing any supranational organisation competent to render verdicts of incontestable authority and enforce absolute submission to the execution of its verdicts. Thus I am led to my first axiom: the quest of international security involves the unconditional surrender by every nation, in a certain measure, of its liberty of action, its sovereignty that is to say, and it is clear beyond all doubt that no other road can lead to such security.

The ill-success, despite their obvious sincerity, of all the efforts made during the last decade to reach this goal leaves us no room to doubt that strong psychological factors are at work, which paralyse these efforts. Some of these factors are not far to seek. The craving for power which characterises the governing class in every nation is hostile to any limitation of the national sovereignty. This political power-hunger is wont to batten on the activities of another group, whose aspirations are on purely mercenary, economic lines. I have specially in mind that small but determined group, active in every nation, composed of individuals who, indifferent to social considerations and restraints, regard warfare, the manufacture and sale of arms, simply as an occasion to advance their personal interests and enlarge their personal authority.

But recognition of this obvious fact is merely the first step towards an appreciation of the actual state of affairs. Another question follows hard upon it: How is it possible for this small clique to bend the will of the majority, who stand to lose and suffer by a state of war, to the service of their ambitions? (In speaking of the majority, I do not exclude soldiers of every rank who have chosen war as their profession, in the belief that they are serving to def end the highest interests of their race, and that attack is often the best method of defence.) An obvious answer to this question would seem to be that the minority, the ruling class at present, has the schools and press, usually the Church as well, under its thumb. This enables it to organise and sway the emotions of the masses, and make its tool of them.

Yet even this answer does not provide a complete solution. Another question arises from it: How is it these devices succeed so well in rousing men to such wild enthusiasm, even to sacrifice their lives? Only one answer is possible. Because man has within him a lust for hatred and destruction. In normal times this passion exists in a latent state, it emerges only in unusual circumstances; but it is a comparatively easy task to call it into play and raise it to the power of a collective psychosis. Here lies, perhaps, the crux of all the complex of factors we are considering, an enigma that only the expert in the lore of human instincts can resolve.

And so we come to our last question. Is it possible to control man's mental evolution so as to make him proof against the psychoses of hate and destructiveness? Here I am thinking by no means only of the so-called uncultured masses. Experience proves that it is rather the so-called "lntelligentzia" that is most apt to yield to these disastrous collective suggestions, since the intellectual has no direct contact with life in the raw, but encounters it in its easiest, synthetic form—upon the printed page.

To conclude: I have so far been speaking only of wars between nations; what are known as international conflicts.

But I am well aware that the aggressive instinct operates under other forms and in other circumstances. (I am thinking of civil wars, for instance, due in earlier days to religious zeal, but nowadays to social factors; or, again, the persecution of racial minorities.) But my insistence on what is the most typical, most cruel and extravagant form of conflict between man and man was deliberate, for here we have the best occasion of discovering ways and means to render all armed conflicts impossible.

I know that in your writings we may find answers, explicit or implied, to all the issues of this urgent and absorbing problem. But it would be of the greatest service to us all were you to present the problem of world peace in the light of your most recent discoveries, for such a presentation well might blaze the trail for new and fruitful modes of action.

Yours very sincerely,

EINSTEIN.

SIGMUND FREUD

Vienna, September, 1932.

Dear Professor Einstein,

When I learnt of your intention to invite me to a mutual exchange of views upon a subject which not only interested you personally but seemed deserving, too, of public interest, I cordially assented. I expected you to choose a problem lying on the borderland of the knowable, as it stands today, a theme which each of us, physicist and psychologist, might approach from his own angle, to meet at last on common ground, though setting out from different premises. Thus the question which you put me—what is to be done to rid mankind of the war-menace?—took me by surprise. And, next, I was dumbfounded by the thought of my (of *our,* I almost wrote) incompetence ; for this struck me as being a matter of practical politics, the statesman's proper study. But then I realised that you did not raise the question in your capacity of scientist or physicist, but as a lover of his fellow men, who responded to the call of the League of Nations much as Fridtjof Nansen, the Polar explorer, took on himself the task of succouring homeless and starving victims of the World War. And, next, I reminded myself that I was not being called on to formulate practical proposals, but, rather, to explain how this question of preventing wars strikes a psychologist.

But here, too, you have stated the gist of the matter in your letter—and taken the wind out of my sails! Still, I will gladly follow in your wake and content myself with endorsing your conclusions, which, however, I propose to amplify to the best of my knowledge or surmise.

You begin with the relations between Might and Right, and this is assuredly the proper starting-point for our enquiry. But, for the term "might," I would substitute a tougher and more telling word: "violence." In right and violence we have today an obvious antinomy. It is easy to prove that one has evolved from the other and, when we go back to origins and examine primitive conditions, the solution of the problem follows easily enough. I must crave your indulgence if in what follows I speak of well-known, admitted facts as though they were new *data;* the context necessitates this method.

Conflicts of interest between man and man are resolved, in principle, by the recourse to violence. It is the same in the animal kingdom, from which man cannot claim exclusion; nevertheless men are also prone to conflicts of opinion, touching, on occasion, the loftiest peaks of abstract thought, which seem to call for settlement by quite another method. This refinement is, however, a late development. To start with, brute force was the factor which, in small communities, decided points of ownership and the question which man's will was to prevail. Very soon physical force was implemented, then replaced, by the use of various adjuncts; he proved the victor whose weapon was the better, or handled the more skilfully. Now, for the first time, with the coming of weapons, superior brains began to oust brute force, but the object of the conflict remained the same: one party was to be constrained, by the injury done him or impairment of his strength, to retract a claim or a refusal. This end is most effectively gained when the opponent is definitively put out of action—in other words, is killed. This procedure has two advantages; the enemy cannot renew hostilities, and, secondly, his fate deters others from following his example. Moreover, the slaughter of a foe gratifies an instinctive craving—a point to which we shall revert hereafter. However, another consideration may be set off against this will to kill: the possibility of using an enemy for servile tasks if his spirit be broken and his life spared. Here violence finds an outlet not in slaughter but in subjugation. Hence springs the practice of giving quarter; but the victor, having from now on to reckon with the craving for revenge that rankles in his victim, forfeits to some extent his personal security.

Thus, under primitive conditions, it is superior force—brute violence, or violence backed by arms—that lords it everywhere. We know that in the course of evolution this state of things was modified, a path was traced that led away from violence to law. But what was this path? Surely it issued from a single verity; that the superiority of one strong man can be overborne by an alliance of many weaklings, that *l'union fail la force.* Brute force is overcome by union, the allied might of scattered units makes good its right against the isolated giant. Thus we may define "right" (i.e. law) as the might of a community. Yet it, too, is nothing else than violence, quick to attack whatever individual stands in its path, and it employs the selfsame methods, follows like ends, with but one difference; it is the communal, not individual, violence that has its way. But, for the transition from crude violence to the reign of law, a certain psychological condition must first obtain. The union of the majority must be stable and enduring. If its sole *raison d'etre* be the discomfiture of some overweening individual and, after his downfall, it be dissolved, it leads to nothing. Some other man, trusting to his superior power, will seek to reinstate the rule of violence and the cycle will repeat itself unendingly. Thus the union of the people must be permanent and well organised; it must enact rules to meet the risk of possible revolts; must set up machinery ensuring that its rules—the laws—are observed and that such acts of violence as the laws demand are duly carried out. This recognition of a community of interests engenders among the members of the group a sentiment of unity and fraternal solidarity which constitutes its real strength.

So far I have set out what seems to me the kernel of the matter: the suppression of brute force by the transfer of power to a larger combination, founded on the community of sentiments linking up its members. All the rest is mere tautology and glosses. Now the position is simple enough so long as the community consists of a number of equipollent individuals. The laws of such a group can determine to what extent the individual must forfeit his personal freedom, the right of using personal force as an instrument of violence, to ensure the safety of the group. But such a combination is only theoretically possible; in practice the situation is always complicated by the fact that, from the outset, the group includes elements of unequal power, men and women, elders and children, and, very soon, as a result of war and conquest, victors and the vanquished—i.e. masters and slaves— as well. From this time on the common law takes notice of these inequalities of power, laws are made by and for the rulers, giving the servile classes fewer rights. Thenceforward there exist within the state two factors making for legal instability, but legislative evolution, too: first, the attempts by members of the ruling class to set themselves above the law's restrictions and, secondly, the constant struggle of the ruled to extend their rights and see each gain embodied in the code, replacing legal disabilities by equal laws for all. The second of these tendencies will be particularly marked when there takes place a positive mutation of the balance of power within the community, the frequent outcome of certain historical conditions. In such cases the laws may gradually be adjusted to the changed conditions or (as more usually ensues) the ruling class is loath to reckon with the new developments, the result being insurrections and civil wars, a period when law is in abeyance and force once more the arbiter, followed by a new regime of law. There is another factor of constitutional change, which operates in a wholly pacific manner, viz.: the cultural evolution of the mass of the community; this factor, however, is of a different order and can only be dealt with later.

Thus we see that, even within the group itself, the exercise of violence cannot be avoided when conflicting interests are at stake. But the common needs and habits of men who live in fellowship under the same sky favour a speedy issue of such conflicts and, this being so, the possibilities of peaceful solutions make steady progress. Yet the most casual glance at world-history will show an unending series of conflicts between one community and another or a group of others, between large and smaller units, between cities, countries, races, tribes and kingdoms, almost all of which were settled by the ordeal of war. Such war ends either in pillage or in conquest and its fruits, the downfall of the loser. No single all-embracing judgment can be passed on these wars of aggrandisement. Some, like the war between the Mongols and the Turks, have led to unmitigated misery; others, however, have furthered the transition from violence to law, since they brought larger units into being, within whose limits a recourse to violence was banned and a new regime determined all disputes. Thus the Roman conquests brought that boon, the *pax romana,* to the Mediterranean lands. The French kings' lust for aggrandisement created a new France, flourishing in peace and unity. Paradoxical as it sounds, we must admit that warfare well might serve to pave the way to that unbroken peace we so desire, for it is war that brings vast empires into being, within whose frontiers all warfare is proscribed by a strong central power. In practice, however, this end is not attained, for as a rule the fruits of victory are but short-lived, the new-created unit falls asunder once again, generally because there can be no true cohesion between the parts that violence has welded. Hitherto, moreover, such conquests have only led to aggregations which, for all their magnitude, had limits, and disputes between these units could be resolved only by recourse to arms. For humanity at large the sole result of all these military enterprises was that, instead of frequent not to say incessant, little wars, they had now to face great wars which, for all they came less often, were so much the more destructive. Regarding the world of today the same conclusion holds good, and you, too, have reached it, though by a shorter path. There is but one sure way of ending war and that is the establishment, by common consent, of a central control which shall have the last word in every conflict of interests. For this, two things are needed: first, the creation of such a supreme court of judicature; secondly, its investment with adequate executive force. Unless this second requirement be fulfilled, the first is unavailing. Obviously the League of Nations, acting as a Supreme Court, fulfils the first condition; it does not fulfil the second. It has no force at its disposal and can only get it if the members of the new body, its constituent nations, furnish it. And, as things are, this is a forlorn hope. Still we should be taking a very short-sighted view of the League of Nations were we to ignore the fact that here is an experiment the like of which has rarely-never before, perhaps, on such a scale-been attempted in the course of history. It is an attempt to acquire the authority (in other words, coercive influence), which hitherto reposed exclusively on the possession of power, by calling into play certain idealistic attitudes of mind. We have seen that there are two factors of cohesion in a community: violent compulsion and ties of sentiment ("identifications," in technical parlance) between the members of the group. If one of these factors becomes inoperative, the other may still suffice to hold the group together. Obviously such notions as these can only be significant when they are the expression of a deeply rooted sense of unity, shared by all. It is necessary, therefore, to gauge the efficacy of such sentiments. History tells us that, on occasion, they have been effective. For example, the Panhellenic conception, the Greeks' awareness of superiority over their barbarian neighbours, which found expression in the Amphictyonies, the Oracles and Games, was strong enough to humanise the methods of warfare as between Greeks, though inevitably it failed to prevent conflicts between different elements of the Hellenic race or even to deter a city or group of cities from joining forces with their racial foe, the Persians, for the discomfiture of a rival. The solidarity of Christendom in the Renaissance age was no more effective, despite its vast authority, in hindering Christian nations, large and small alike, from calling in the Sultan to their aid. And, in our times we look in vain for some such unifying notion whose authority would be unquestioned. It is all too clear that the nationalistic ideas, paramount today in every country, operate in quite a contrary direction. Some there are who hold that the Bolshevist conceptions may make an end of war, but, as things are, that goal lies very far away and, perhaps, could only be attained after a spell of brutal internecine warfare. Thus it would seem that any effort to replace brute force by the might of an ideal is, under present conditions, doomed to fail. Our logic is at fault if we ignore the fact that right is founded on brute force and even today needs violence to maintain it.

I now can comment on another of your statements. You are amazed that it is so easy to infect men with the war-fever, and you surmise that man has in him an active instinct for hatred and destruction, amenable to such stimulations. I entirely agree with you. I believe in the existence of this instinct and have been recently at pains to study its manifestations. In this connexion may I set out a fragment of that knowledge of the instincts, which we psychoanalysts, after so many tentative essays and gropings in the dark, have compassed? We assume that human instincts are of two kinds: those that conserve and unify, which we call "erotic" (in the meaning Plato gives to *Eros* in his *Symposium),* or else "sexual" (explicitly extending the popular connotation of "sex"); and, secondly, the instincts to destroy and kill, which we assimilate as the aggressive or destructive instincts. These are, as you perceive, the well-known opposites, Love and Hate, transformed into theoretical entities; they are, perhaps, another aspect of those eternal polarities, attraction and repulsion, which fall within your province. But we must be chary of passing over-hastily to the notions of good and evil. Each of these instincts is every whit as indispensable as its opposite and all the phenomena of life derive from their activity, whether they work in concert or in opposition. It seems that an instinct of either category can operate but rarely in isolation; it is always blended ("alloyed," as we say) with a certain dosage of its opposite, which modifies its aim or even, in certain circumstances, is a prime condition of its attainment. Thus the instinct of self-preservation is certainly of an erotic nature, but to gain its ends this very instinct necessitates aggressive action. In the same way the love-instinct, when directed to a specific object, calls for an admixture of the acquisitive instinct if it is to enter into effective possession of that object. It is the difficulty of isolating the two kinds of instinct in their manifestations that has so long prevented us from recognising them.

If you will travel with me a little further on this road, you will find that human affairs are complicated in yet another way. Only exceptionally does an action follow on the stimulus of a single instinct, which is per se a blend of Eros and destructiveness. As a rule several motives of similar composition concur to bring about the act. This fact was duly noted by a colleague of yours, Professor G. C. Lichtenberg, sometime Professor of Physics at Gottingen; he was perhaps even more eminent as a psychologist than as a physical scientist. He evolved the notion of a " Compass-card of Motives" and wrote: " The efficient motives impelling man to act can be classified like the 32 Winds, and described in the same manner ; e.g. Food-Food-Fame or Fame-Fame-Food." Thus, when a nation is summoned to engage in war, a whole gamut of human motives may respond to this appeal; high and low motives, some openly avowed, others slurred over. The lust for aggression and destruction is certainly included; the innumerable cruelties of history and man's daily life confirm its prevalence and strength. The stimulation of these destructive impulses by appeals to idealism and the erotic instinct naturally facilitates their release. Musing on the atrocities recorded on history's page, we feel that the ideal motive has often served as a camouflage for the lust of destruction; sometimes, as with the cruelties of the Inquisition, it seems that, while the ideal motives occupied the foreground of consciousness, they drew their strength from the destructive instincts submerged in the unconscious. Both interpretations are feasible.

You are interested, I know, in the prevention of war, not in our theories, and I keep this fact in mind. Yet I would like to dwell a little longer on this destructive instinct which is seldom given the attention that its importance warrants. With the least of speculative efforts we are led to conclude that this instinct functions in every living being, striving to work its ruin and reduce life to its primal state of inert matter. Indeed it might well be called the "death-instinct";

whereas the erotic instincts vouch for the struggle to live on. The death instinct becomes an impulse to destruction when, with the aid of certain organs, it directs its action outwards, against external objects. The living being, that is to say, defends its own existence by destroying foreign bodies. But, in one of its activities, the death instinct is operative *within* the living being and we have sought to trace back a number of normal and pathological phenomena to this *intro-ursion* of the destructive instinct. We have even committed the heresy of explaining the origin of human conscience by some such "turning inward" of the aggressive impulse. Obviously when this internal tendency operates on too large a scale, it is no trivial matter, rather a positively morbid state of things; whereas the diversion of the destructive impulse towards the external world must have beneficial effects. Here is then the biological justification for all those vile, pernicious propensities which we now are combating. We can but own that they are really more akin to nature than this our stand against them, which, in fact, remains to be accounted for.

All this may give you the impression that our theories amount to a species of mythology and a gloomy one at that! But does not every natural science lead ultimately to this—a sort of mythology? Is it otherwise today with your physical science?

The upshot of these observations, as bearing on the subject in hand, is that there is no likelihood of our being able to suppress humanity's aggressive tendencies. In some happy corners of the earth, they say, where nature brings forth abundantly whatever man desires, there flourish races whose lives go gently by, unknowing of aggression or constraint.

This I can hardly credit; I would like further details about these happy folk. The Bolshevists, too, aspire to do away with human aggressiveness by ensuring the satisfaction of material needs and enforcing equality between man and man. To me this hope seems vain. Meanwhile they busily perfect their armaments, and their hatred of outsiders is not the least of the factors of cohesion amongst themselves. In any case, as you too have observed, complete suppression of man's aggressive tendencies is not in issue; what we may try is to divert it into a channel other than that of warfare.

From our "mythology" of the instincts we may easily deduce a formula for an indirect method of eliminating war. If the propensity for war be due to the destructive instinct, we have always its counter-agent, Eros, to our hand. All that produces ties of sentiment between man and man must serve us as war's antidote. These ties are of two kinds. First, such relations as those towards a beloved object, void though they be of sexual intent. The psychoanalyst need feel no compunction in mentioning "love" in this connexion; religion uses the same language: Love thy neighbour as thyself. A pious injunction easy to enounce, but hard to carry out! The other bond of sentiment is by way of identification. All that brings out the significant resemblances between men calls into play this feeling of community, identification, whereon is founded, in large measure, the whole edifice of human society.

In your strictures on the abuse of authority I find another suggestion for an indirect attack on the war-impulse. That men are divided into leaders and the led is but another manifestation of their inborn and irremediable inequality. The second class constitutes the vast majority; they need a high command to make decisions for them, to which decisions they usually bow without demur. In this context we would point out that men should be at greater pains than heretofore to form a superior class of independent thinkers, unamenable to intimidation and fervent in the quest of truth, whose function it would be to guide the masses dependent on their lead. There is no need to point out how little the rule of politicians and the Church's ban on liberty of thought encourage such a new creation. The ideal conditions would obviously be found in a community where every man subordinated his instinctive life to the dictates of reason. Nothing less than this could bring about so thorough and so durable a union between men, even if this involved the severance of mutual ties of sentiment. But surely such a hope is utterly utopian, as things are. The other indirect methods of preventing war are certainly more feasible, but entail no quick results. They conjure up an ugly picture of mills that grind so slowly that, before the flour is ready, men are dead of hunger.

As you see, little good comes of consulting a theoretician, aloof from worldly contacts, on practical and urgent problems! Better it were to tackle each successive crisis with means that we have ready to our hands. However, I would like to deal with a question which, though it is not mooted in your letter, interests me greatly. Why do we, you and I and many an other, protest so vehemently against war, instead of just accepting it as another of life's odious importunities? For it seems a natural thing enough, biologically sound and practically unavoidable. I trust you will not be shocked by my raising such a question. For the better conduct of an inquiry it may be well to don a mask of feigned aloofness. The answer to my query may run as follows: Because every man has a right over his own life and war destroys lives that were full of promise; it forces the individual into situations that shame his manhood, obliging him to murder fellow men, against his will; it ravages material amenities, the fruits of human toil, and much besides. Moreover wars, as now conducted, afford no scope for acts of heroism according to the old ideals and, given the high perfection of modern arms, war today would mean the sheer extermination of one of the combatants, if not of both. This is so true, so obvious, that we can but wonder why the conduct of war is not banned by general consent. Doubtless either of the points I have just made is open to debate. It may be asked if the community, in its turn, cannot claim a right over the individual lives of its members. Moreover, all forms of war cannot be indiscriminately condemned; so long as there are nations and empires, each prepared callously to exterminate its rival, all alike must be equipped for war. But we will not dwell on any of these problems; they lie outside the debate to which you have invited me. I pass on to another point, the basis, as it strikes me, of our common hatred of war. It is this: we cannot do otherwise than hate it. Pacifists we are, since our organic nature wills us thus to be. Hence it comes easy to us to find arguments that justify our standpoint.

This point, however, calls for elucidation. Here is the way in which I see it. The cultural development of mankind (some, I know, prefer to call it civilisation) has been in progress since immemorial antiquity. To this processus we owe all that is best in our composition, but also much that makes for human suffering. Its origins and causes are obscure, its issue is uncertain, but some of its characteristics are easy to perceive. It well may lead to the extinction of mankind, for it impairs the sexual function in more than one respect, and even today the uncivilised races and the backward classes of all nations are multiplying more rapidly than the cultured elements. This process may, perhaps, be likened to the effects of domestication on certain animals— it clearly involves physical changes of structure—but the view that cultural development is an organic process of this order has not yet become generally familiar. The psychic changes which accompany this process of cultural change are striking, and not to be gainsaid. They consist in the progressive rejection of instinctive ends and a scaling down of instinctive reactions. Sensations which delighted our forefathers have become neutral or unbearable to us; and, if our ethical and aesthetic ideals have undergone a change, the causes of this are ultimately organic. On the psychological side two of the most important phenomena of culture are, firstly, a strengthening of the intellect, which tends to master our instinctive life, and, secondly, an introversion of the aggressive impulse, with all its consequent benefits and perils. Now war runs most emphatically counter to the psychic disposition imposed on us by the growth of culture; we are therefore bound to resent war, to find it utterly intolerable. With pacifists like us it is not merely an intellectual and affective repulsion, but a constitutional intolerance, an idiosyncrasy in its most drastic form. And it would seem that the aesthetic ignominies of warfare play almost as large a part in this repugnance as war's atrocities.

How long have we to wait before the rest of men turn pacifist? Impossible to say, and yet perhaps our hope that these two factors—man's cultural disposition and a well-founded dread of the form that future wars will take—may serve to put an end to war in the near future, is not chimerical. But by what ways or by-ways this will come about, we cannot guess. Meanwhile we may rest on the assurance that whatever makes for cultural development is working also against war.

With kindest regards and, should this expose prove a disappointment to you, my sincere regrets,

Yours,

SIGMUND FREUD.

THOUGHTS FOR THE TIMES
ON WAR AND DEATH
by Sigmund Freud

I

THE DISILLUSIONMENT OF THE WAR

I N THE CONFUSION of wartime in which we are caught up, relying as we must on one-sided information, standing too close to the great changes that have already taken place or are beginning to, and without a glimmering of the future that is being shaped, we ourselves are at a loss as to the significance of the impressions which press in upon us and as to the value of the judgements which we form. We cannot but feel that no event has ever destroyed so much that is precious in the common possessions of humanity, confused so many of the clearest intelligences, or so thoroughly debased what is highest. Science herself has lost her passionless impartiality; her deeply embittered servants seek for weapons from her with which to contribute towards the struggle with the enemy. Anthropologists feel driven to declare him inferior and degenerate, psychiatrists issue a diagnosis of his disease of mind or spirit. Probably, however, our sense of these immediate evils is disproportionately strong, and we are not entitled to compare them with the evils of other times which we have not experienced.

The individual who is not himself a combatant—and so a cog in the gigantic machine of war—feels bewildered in his orientation, and inhibited in his powers and activities. I believe that he will welcome any indication, however slight, which will make it easier for him to find his bearings within himself at least. I propose to pick out two among the factors which are responsible for the mental distress felt by non-combatants, against which it is such a heavy task to struggle, and to treat of them here: the disillusionment which this war has evoked, and the altered attitude towards death which this—like every other war—forces upon us.

When I speak of disillusionment, everyone will know at once what I mean. One need not be a sentimentalist; one may perceive the biological and psychological necessity for suffering in the economy of human life, and yet condemn war both in its means and ends and long for the cessation of all wars. We have told ourselves, no doubt, that wars can never cease so long as nations live under such widely differing conditions, so long as the value of individual life is so variously assessed among them, and so long as the animosities which divide them represent such powerful motive forces in the mind. We were prepared to find that wars between the primitive and the civilized peoples, between the races who are divided by the colour of their skin—wars, even, against and among the nationalities of Europe whose civilization is little developed or has been lost—would occupy mankind for some time to come. But we permitted ourselves to have other hopes. We had expected the great world-dominating nations of white race upon whom the leadership of the human species has fallen, who were known to have world-wide interests as their concern, to whose creative powers were due not only our technical advances towards the control of nature but the artistic and scientific standards of civilization—we had expected these peoples to succeed in discovering another way of settling misunderstandings and conflicts of interest. Within each of these nations high norms of moral conduct were laid down for the individual, to which his manner of life was bound to conform if he desired to take part in a civilized community. These ordinances, often too stringent, demanded a great deal of him—much self-restraint, much renunciation of instinctual satisfaction. He was above all forbidden to make use of the immense advantages to be gained by the practice of lying and deception in the competition with his fellow-men. The civilized states regarded these moral standards as the basis of their existence. They took serious steps if anyone ventured to tamper with them, and often declared it improper even to subject them to examination by a critical intelligence. It was to be assumed, therefore, that the state itself would respect them, and would not think of undertaking anything against them which would contradict the basis of its own existence. Observation showed, to be sure, that embedded in these civilized states there were remnants of certain other peoples, which were universally unpopular and had therefore been only reluctantly, and even so not fully, admitted to participation in the common work of civilization, for which they had shown themselves suitable enough. But the great nations themselves, it might have been supposed, would have acquired so much comprehension of what they had in common, and so much tolerance for their differences, that "foreigner" and "enemy" could no longer be merged, as they still were in classical antiquity, into a single concept.

Relying on this unity among the civilized peoples, count-less men and women have exchanged their native home for a foreign one, and made their existence dependent on the intercommunications between friendly nations. Moreover anyone who was not by stress of circumstance confined to one spot could create for himself out of all the advan-tages and attractions of these civilized countries a new and wider fatherland, in which he could move about without hindrance or suspicion. In this way he enjoyed the blue sea and the grey; the beauty of snow-covered mountains and of green meadow lands; the magic of northern forests and the splendour of southern vegetation; the mood evoked by landscapes that recall great historical events, and the silence of untouched nature. This new fatherland was a museum for him, too, filled with all the treasures which the artists of civilized humanity had in the successive centuries created and left behind. As he wandered from one gallery to another in this museum, he could recognize with impartial appre-ciation what varied types of perfection a mixture of blood, the course of history, and the special quality of their moth-er-earth had produced among his compatriots in this wider sense. Here he would find cool, inflexible energy developed to the highest point; there, the graceful art of beautifying existence; elsewhere, the feeling for orderliness and law, or others among the qualities which have made mankind the lords of the earth.

Nor must we forget that each of these citizens of the civilized world had created for himself a "Parnassus" and a "School of Athens" of his own. From among the great think-ers, writers and artists of all nations he had chosen those to whom he considered he owed the best of what he had been able to achieve in enjoyment and understanding of life, and he had venerated them along with the immortal ancients as well as with the familiar masters of his own tongue. None of these great men had seemed to him foreign because they spoke another language—neither the incomparable explorer of human passions, nor the intoxicated worshipper of beauty, nor the powerful and menacing prophet, nor the subtle satirist; and he never reproached himself on that account for being a renegade towards his own nation and his beloved mother-tongue.

The enjoyment of this common civilization was disturbed from time to time by warning voices, which declared that old traditional differences made wars inevitable, even among the members of a community such as this. We refused to believe it; but if such a war were to happen, how did we picture it? We saw it as an opportunity for demonstrating the progress of comity among men since the era when the Greek Amphictyonic Council proclaimed that no city of the league might be destroyed, nor its olive-groves cut down, nor its water-supply stopped; we pictured it as a chivalrous passage of arms, which would limit itself to establishing the superiority of one side in the struggle, while as far as possible avoiding acute suffering that could contribute nothing to the decision, and granting complete immunity for the wounded who had to withdraw from the contest, as well as for the doctors and nurses who devoted themselves to their recovery. There would, of course, be the utmost consideration for the non-combatant classes of the population—for women who take no part in war-work, and for the children who, when they are grown up, should become on both sides one another's friends and helpers. And again, all the international undertakings and institutions in which the common civilization of peace-time had been embodied would be maintained.

Even a war like this would have produced enough horror and suffering; but it would not have interrupted the development of ethical relations between the collective individuals of mankind-the peoples and states.

Then the war in which we had refused to believe broke out, and it brought—disillusionment. Not only is it more bloody and more destructive than any war of other days, because of the enormously increased perfection of weapons of attack and defence; it is at least as cruel, as embittered, as implacable as any that has preceded it. It disregards all the restrictions known as International Law, which in peace-time the states had bound themselves to observe; it ignores the prerogatives of the wounded and the medical service, the distinction between civil and military sections of the population, the claims of private property. It tramples in blind fury on all that comes in its way, as though there were to be no future and no peace among men after it is over. It cuts all the common bonds between the contending peoples, and threatens to leave a legacy of embitterment that will make any renewal of those bonds impossible for a long time to come.

Moreover, it has brought to light an almost incredible phenomenon: the civilized nations know and understand one another so little that one can turn against the other with hate and loathing. Indeed, one of the great civilized nations is so universally unpopular that the attempt can actually be made to exclude it from the civilized community as "barbaric," although it has long proved its fitness by the magnificent contributions to that community which it has made. We live in hopes that the pages of an impartial history will prove that that nation, in whose language we write and for whose victory our dear ones are fighting, has been precisely the one which has least transgressed the laws of civilization. But at such a time who dares to set himself up as judge in his own cause?

Peoples are more or less represented by the states which they form, and these states by the governments which rule them. The individual citizen can with horror convince himself in this war of what would occasionally cross his mind in peace-time—that the state has forbidden to the individual the practice of wrong-doing, not because it desires to abolish it, but because it desires to monopolize it, like salt and tobacco. A belligerent state permits itself every such misdeed, every such act of violence, as would disgrace the individual. It makes use against the enemy not only the accepted *ruses de guerre,* but of deliberate lying and deception as well—and to a degree which seems to exceed the usage of former wars. The state exacts the utmost degree of obedience and sacrifice from its citizens, but at the same time it treats them like children by an excess of secrecy and a censorship upon news and expressions of opinion which leaves the spirits of those whose intellects it thus suppresses defenceless against every unfavourable turn of events and every sinister rumour. It absolves itself from the guarantees and treaties by which it was bound to other states, and confesses shamelessly to its own rapacity and lust for power, which the private individual has then to sanction in the name of patriotism.

It should not be objected that the state cannot refrain from wrong-doing, since that would place it at a disadvantage. It

is no less disadvantageous, as a general rule, for the individual man to conform to the standards of morality and refrain
from brutal and arbitrary conduct; and the state seldom
proves able to indemnify him for the sacrifices it exacts. Nor
should it be a matter for surprise that this relaxation of all
the moral ties between the collective individuals of mankind
should have had repercussions on the morality of individuals; for our conscience is not the inflexible judge that ethical
teachers declare it, but in its origin is "social anxiety" and
nothing else. When the com-munity no longer raises objec-
tions, there is an end, too, to the suppression of evil passions, and men perpetrate deeds of cruelty, fraud, treachery,
and barbarity so incompatible with their level of civilization
that one would have thought them impossible.

Well may the citizen of the civilized world of whom I have
spoken stand helpless in a world that has grown strange to
him—his great fatherland disintegrated, its common estates
laid waste, his fellow-citizens divided and debased!

There is something to be said, however, in criticism of
his disappointment. Strictly speaking it is not justified, for
it consists in the destruction of an illusion. We welcome
illusions because they spare us unpleasurable feelings, and
enable us to enjoy satisfactions instead. We must not com-
plain, then, if now and again they come into collision with
some portion of reality, and are shattered against it.

Two things in this war have aroused our sense of disillusionment: the low morality shown externally by states which
in their internal relations pose as the guardians of moral
standards, and the brutality shown by individuals whom,
as participants in the highest human civilization, one would
not have thought capable of such behaviour.

Let us begin with the second point and try to formulate, in a few brief words, the point of view that we wish to criticize. How, in point of fact, do we imagine the process by which an individual rises to a comparatively high plane of morality? The first answer will no doubt simply be that he is virtuous and noble from birth—from the very start. We shall not consider this view any further here. A second answer will suggest that we are concerned with a developmental process, and will probably assume that the development consists in eradicating his evil human tendencies and, under the influence of education and a civilized environment, replacing them by good ones. If so, it is nevertheless surprising that evil should re-emerge with such force in anyone who has been brought up in this way.

But this answer also contains the thesis which we propose to contradict. In reality, there is no such thing as "eradicating" evil. Psychological—or, more strictly speaking, psycho-analytic—investigation shows instead that the deepest essence of human nature consists of instinctual impulses which are of an elementary nature, which are similar in all men and which aim at the satisfaction of certain primal needs. These impulses in themselves are neither good nor bad. We classify them and their expressions in that way, according to their relation to the needs and demands of the human community. It must be granted that all the impulses which society condemns as evil—let us take as representative the selfish and the cruel ones—are of this primitive kind.

These primitive impulses undergo a lengthy process of development before they are allowed to become active in the adult. They are inhibited, directed towards other aims and fields, become commingled, alter their objects, and are to some extent turned back upon their possessor. Reaction-formations against certain instincts take the deceptive form of a change in their content, as though egoism had changed into altruism, or cruelty into pity. These reaction-formations are facilitated by the circumstance that some instinctual impulses make their appearance almost from the first in pairs of opposites—a very remarkable phenomenon, and one strange to the lay public, which is termed "ambivalence of feeling." The most easily observed and comprehensible instance of this is the fact that intense love and intense hatred are so often to be found together in the same person. Psycho-analysis adds that the two opposed feelings not infrequently have the same person for their object.

It is not until all these "instinctual vicissitudes" have been surmounted that what we call a person's character is formed, and this, as we know, can only very inadequately be classified as "good" or "bad." A human being is seldom altogether good or bad; he is usually "good" in one relation and "bad" in another, or "good" in certain external circumstances and in others decidedly "bad. It is interesting to find that the pre-existence of strong "bad" impulses in infancy is often the actual condition for an unmistakable inclination towards "good" in the adult. Those who as children have been the most pronounced egoists may well become the most helpful and self-sacrificing members of the community; most of our sentimentalists, friends of humanity, and protectors of animals have been evolved from little sadists and amimal-tormentors.

The transformation of "bad" instincts is brought about by two factors working in the same direction, an internal and an external one. The internal factor consists in the influence exercised on the bad (let us say, the egoistic) instincts by erotism—that is, by the human need for love, taken in its widest sense. By the admixture of *erotic* components the egoistic instincts are transformed into *social* ones. We learn to value being loved as an advantage for which we are willing to sacrifice other advantages. The external factor is the force exercised by upbringing, which represents the claims of our cultural environment, and this is continued later by the direct pressure of that environment. Civilization has been attained through the renunciation of instinctual satisfaction, and it demands the same renunciation from each newcomer in turn. Throughout an individual's life there is a constant replacement of external by internal compulsion. The influences of civilization cause an ever-increasing transformation of egoistic trends into altruistic and social ones by an admixture of erotic elements. In the last resort it may be assumed that every internal compulsion which makes itself felt in the development of human beings was originally—that is, in the *history of mankind*—only an external one. Those who are born today bring with them as an inherited organization some degree of tendency (disposition) towards the transformation of egoistic into social instincts, and this disposition is easily stimulated into bringing about that result. A further portion of this instinctual transformation has to be accomplished during the life of the individual himself. So the human being is subject not only to the pressure of his immediate cultural environment, but also to the influence of the cultural history of his ancestors.

If we give the name of "susceptibility to culture" to a man's personal capacity for the transformation of the egoistic impulses under the influence of erotism, we may further affirm that this susceptibility is made up of two parts, one innate and the other acquired in the course of life, and that the relation of the two to each other and to that portion of the instinctual life which remains untransformed is a very variable one.

Generally speaking, we are apt to attach too much importance to the innate part, and in addition to this we run the risk of over-estimating the total susceptibility to culture in comparison with the portion of instinctual life which has remained primitive—that is, we are misled into regarding men as "better" than they actually are. For there is yet another element which obscures our judgement and falsifies the issue in a favourable sense.

The instinctual impulses of other people are of course hidden from our observation. We infer them from their actions and behaviour, which we trace back to *motives* arising from their instinctual life. Such an inference is bound to be erroneous in many cases. This or that action which is "good" from the cultural point of view may in one instance originate from a "noble" motive, in another not. Ethical theorists class as "good" actions only those which are the outcome of good impulses; to the others they refuse recognition. But society, which is practical in its aims, is not on the whole troubled by this distinction; it is content if a man regulates his behaviour and actions by the precepts of civilization, and is little concerned with his motives.

We have learned that the *external compulsion* exercised on a human being by his upbringing and environment produces a further transformation towards good in his instinctual life—a, further turning from egoism towards altruism. But this is not the regular or necessary effect of the external compulsion. Upbringing and environment not only offer benefits in the way of love, but also employ other kinds of incentive, namely, rewards and punishments. In this way their effect may tum out to be that a person who is subjected to their influence will choose to behave well in the cultural sense of the phrase, although no ennoblement of instinct, no transformation of egoistic into altruistic inclinations, has taken place in him. The result will, roughly speaking, be the same; only a particular concatenation of circumstances will reveal that one man always acts in a good way because his instinctual inclinations compel him to, and the other is good only in so far and for so long as such cultural behaviour is advantageous for his own selfish purposes. But superficial acquaintance with an individual will not enable us to distinguish between the two cases, and we are certainly misled by our optimism into grossly exaggerating the number of human beings who have been transformed in a cultural sense.

Civilized society, which demands good conduct and does not trouble itself about the instinctual basis of this conduct, has thus won over to obedience a great many people who are not in this following their own natures. Encouraged by this success, society has allowed itself to be misled into tightening the moral standard to the greatest possible degree, and it has thus forced its members into a yet greater estrangement from their instinctual disposition. They are consequently subject to an unceasing suppression of instinct, and the resulting tension betrays itself in the most remarkable phenomena of reaction and compensation. In the domain of sexuality, where such suppression is most difficult to carry out, the result is seen in the reactive phenomena of neurotic disorders. Elsewhere the pressure of civilization brings in its train no pathological results, it is true, but is shown in malformations of character, and in the perpetual readiness of the inhibited instincts to break through to satisfaction at any suitable opportunity. Anyone thus compelled to act continually in accordance with precepts which are not the expression of his instinctual inclinations, is living, psychologically speaking, beyond his means, and may objectively be described as a hypocrite, whether he is clearly aware of the incongruity or not. It is undeniable that our contemporary civilization favours the production of this form of hypocrisy to an extraordinary extent. One might venture to say that it is built up on such hypocrisy, and that it would have to submit to far-reaching modifications if people were to undertake to live in accordance with psychological truth. Thus there are very many more cultural hypocrites than truly civilized men—indeed, it is a debatable point whether a certain degree of cultural hypocrisy is not indispensable for the maintenance of civilization, because the susceptibility to culture which has hitherto been organized in the minds of present-day men would perhaps not prove sufficient for the task. On the other hand, the maintenance of civilization even on so dubious a basis offers the prospect of paving the way in each new generation for a more far-reaching transformation of instinct which shall be the vehicle of a better civilization.

We may already derive one consolation from this discussion: our mortification and our painful disillusionment on account of the uncivilized behaviour of our fellow-citizens of the world during this war were unjustified. They were based on an illusion to which we had given way. In reality our fellow-citizens have not sunk so low as we feared, because they had never risen so high as we believed. The fact that the collective individuals of mankind, the peoples and states, mutually abrogated their moral restraints naturally prompted these individual citizens to withdraw for a while from the constant pressure of civilization and to grant a temporary satisfaction to the instincts which they had been holding in check. This probably involved no breach in their relative morality within their own nations.

We may, however, obtain a deeper insight than this into the change brought about by the war in our former compatriots, and at the same time receive a warning against doing them an injustice. For the development of the mind shows a peculiarity which is present in no other developmental process. When a village grows into a town or a child into a man, the village and the child, become lost in the town and the man. Memory alone can trace the old features in the new picture; and in fact the old materials or forms have been got rid of and replaced by new ones. It is otherwise with the development of the mind. Here one can describe the state of affairs, which has nothing to compare with it, only by saying that in this case every earlier stage of development persists alongside the later stage which has arisen from it; here succession also involves co-existence, although it is to the same materials that the whole series of transformations has applied. The earlier mental state may not have manifested itself for years, but none the less it is so far present that it may at any time again become the mode of expression of the forces in the mind, and indeed the only one, as though all later developments had been annulled or undone. This extraordinary plasticity of mental developments is not unrestricted as regards direction; it may be described as a special capacity for involution—for regression—since it may well happen that a later and higher stage of development, once abandoned, cannot be reached again. But the primitive stages can always be re-established; the primitive mind is, in the fullest meaning of the word, imperishable.

What are called mental diseases inevitably produce an impression in the layman that intellectual and mental life have been destroyed. In reality, the destruction only applies to later acquisitions and developments. The essence of mental disease lies in a return to earlier states of affective life and of functioning. An excellent example of the plasticity of mental life is afforded by the state of sleep, which is our goal every night. Since we have learnt to interpret even absurd and confused dreams, we know that whenever we go to sleep we throw off our hard-won morality like a garment, and put it on again next morning. This stripping of ourselves is not, of course, dangerous, because we are paralysed, condemned to inactivity, by the state of sleep. It is only dreams that can tell us about the regression of our emotional life to one of the earliest stages of development. For instance, it is noteworthy that all our dreams are governed by purely egoistic motives. One of my English friends put forward this thesis at a scientific meeting in America, whereupon a lady who was present remarked that that might be the case in Austria, but she could assert as regards herself and her friends that *they* were altruistic even in their dreams. My friend, although himself of English race, was obliged to contradict the lady emphatically on the ground of his personal experience in dream-analysis, and to declare that in their dreams high-minded American ladies were quite as egoistic as the Austrians.

Thus the transformation of instinct, on which our susceptibility to culture is based, may also be permanently or temporarily undone by the impacts of life. The influences of war are undoubtedly among the forces that can bring about such involution; so we need not deny susceptibility to culture to all who are at the present time behaving in an uncivilized way, and we may anticipate that the ennoblement of their instincts will be restored in more peaceful times.

There is, however, another symptom in our fellow-citizens of the world which has perhaps astonished and shocked us no less than the descent from their ethical heights which has given us so much pain. What I have in mind is the want of insight shown by the best intellects, their obduracy, their inaccessibility to the most forcible arguments and their uncritical credulity towards the most disputable assertions. This indeed presents a lamentable picture, and I wish to say emphatically that in this I am by no means a blind partisan who finds all the intellectual short-comings on one side. But this phenomenon is much easier to account for and much less disquieting than the one we have just considered. Students of human nature and philosophers have long taught us that we are mistaken in regarding our intelligence as an independent force and in overlooking its dependence on emotional life. Our intellect, they teach us, can function reliably only when it is removed from the influences of strong emotional impulses; otherwise it behaves merely as an instrument of the will and delivers the inference which the will requires. Thus, in their view, logical arguments are impotent against affective interests, and that is why disputes backed by reasons, which in Falstaff's phrase are "as plenty as black-berries," are so unfruitful in the world of interests. Psycho-analytic experience has, if possible, further confirmed this statement. It can show every day that the shrewdest people will all of a sudden behave without insight, like imbeciles, as soon as the necessary insight is confronted by an emo-tional resistance, but that they will completely regain their understanding once that resistance has been overcome. The logical bedazzlement which this war has conjured up in our fellow-citizens, many of them the best of their kind, is there-fore a secondary phenomenon, a consequence of emotional excitement, and is bound, we may hope, to disappear with it.

Having in this way once more come to understand our fellow-citizens who are now alienated from us, we shall much more easily endure the disappointment which the nations, the collective individuals of mankind, have caused us, for the demands we make upon these should be far more modest. Perhaps they are recapitulating the course of indi-vidual development, and today still represent very primitive phases in organization and in the formation of higher uni-ties. It is in agreement with this that the educative factor of an external compulsion towards morality, which we found was so effective in individuals, is as yet barely discernible in them. We had hoped, certainly, that the extensive com-munity of interests established by commerce and produc-tion would constitute the germ of such a compulsion, but it would seem that nations still obey their passions far more readily than their interests. Their interests serve them, at most, as *rationalizations* for their passions; they put for-ward their interests in order to be able to give reasons for satisfying their passions. It is, to be sure, a mystery why the collective individuals should in fact despise, hate and detest one another—every nation against every other—and even in times of peace. I cannot tell why that is so. It is just as though when it becomes a question of a number of people, not to say millions, all individual moral acquisitions are obliterated, and only the most primitive, the oldest, the crudest mental attitudes are left. It may be that only later stages in development will be able to make some change in this regrettable state of affairs. But a little more truthfulness and honesty on all sides—in the relations of men to one another and between them and their rulers—should also smooth the way for this transformation.

II
OUR ATTITUDE TOWARDS DEATH

THE SECOND FACTOR to which I attribute our present sense of estrangement in this once lovely and congenial world is the disturbance that has taken place in the attitude which we have hitherto adopted towards death.

That attitude was far from straightforward. To anyone who listened to us we were of course prepared to maintain that death was the necessary outcome of life, that everyone owes nature a death and must expect to pay the debt—in short, that death was natural, undeniable, and unavoidable. In reality, however, we were accustomed to behave as if it were otherwise. We showed an unmistakable tendency to put death on one side, to eliminate it from life. We tried to hush it up; indeed we even have a saying [in German]: "to think of something as though it were death." That is, as though it were our own death, of course. It is indeed impossible to imagine our own death; and whenever we attempt to do so we can perceive that we are in fact still present as spectators. Hence the psycho-analytic school could venture on the assertion that at bottom no one believes in his own death, or, to put the same thing in another way, that in the unconscious every one of us is convinced of his own immortality.

When it comes to someone else's death, the civilized man will carefully avoid speaking of such a possibility in the hearing of the person under sentence. Children alone disregard this restriction; they unashamedly threaten one another with the possibility of dying, and even go so far as to do the same thing to someone whom they love, as, for instance: "Dear Mummy, when you're dead I'll do this or that." The civilized adult can hardly even entertain the thought of another person's death without seeming to himself hard-hearted or wicked; unless, of course, as a doctor or lawyer or something of the kind, he has to deal with death professionally. Least of all will he allow himself to think of the other person's death if some gain to himself in freedom, property, or position is bound up with it. This sensitiveness of ours does not, of course, prevent the occurrence of deaths; when one does happen, we are always deeply affected, and it is as though we were badly shaken in our expectations. Our habit is to lay stress on the fortuitous causation of the death—accident, disease, infection, advanced age; in this way we betray an effort to reduce death from a necessity to a chance event. A number of simultaneous deaths strikes us as something extremely terrible. Towards the actual person who has died we adopt a special attitude—something almost like admiration for someone who has accomplished a very difficult task. We suspend criticism of him, overlook his possible misdeeds, declare that *"de mortuis nil nisi bonum,"* and think it justifiable to set out all that is most favourable to his memory in the funeral oration and upon the tombstone. Consideration for the dead, who, after all, no longer need it, is more important to us than the truth, and certainly, for most of us, than consideration for the living.

The complement to this cultural and conventional attitude towards death is provided by our complete collapse when death has struck down someone whom we love—a parent or a partner in marriage, a brother or sister, a child, or a close friend. Our hopes, our desires and our pleasures lie in the grave with him, we will not be consoled, we will not fill the lost one's place. We behave as if we were a kind of Asra, who die when those they love die.

But this attitude of ours towards death has a powerful effect on our lives. Life is impoverished, it loses in interest, when the highest stake in the game of living, life itself, may not be risked. It becomes as shallow and empty as, let us say, an American flirtation, in which it is understood from the first that nothing is, to happen, as contrasted with a Continental love-affair in which both partners must constantly bear its serious consequences in mind. Our emotional ties, the unbearable intensity of our grief, make us disinclined to court danger for ourselves and for those who belong to us. We dare not contemplate a great many undertakings which are dangerous but in fact indispensable, such as attempts at artificial flight, expeditions to distant countries, or experiments with explosive substances. We are paralysed by the thought of who is to take the son's place with his mother, the husband's with his wife, the father's with his children, if a disaster should occur. Thus the tendency to exclude death from our calculations in life brings in its train many other renunciations and exclusions. Yet the motto of the Hanseatic League ran: *"Navigare necesse est, vivere non necesse."* ("It is necessary to sail the seas, it is not necessary to live.")

It is an inevitable result of all this that we should seek in the world of fiction, in literature, and in the theatre compensation for what has been lost in life. There we still find people who know how to die—who, indeed, even manage to kill someone else. There alone too the condition can be fulfilled which makes it possible for us to reconcile ourselves with death: namely, that behind all the vicissitudes of life we should still be able to preserve a life intact. For it is really too sad that in life it should be as it is in chess, where one false move may force us to resign the game, but with the difference that we can start no second game, no return-match. In the realm of fiction we find the plurality of lives which we need. We die with the hero with whom we have identified ourselves yet we survive him, and are ready to die again just as safely with another hero.

It is evident that war is bound to sweep away this conventional treatment of death. Death will no longer be denied; we are forced to believe in it. People really die; and no longer one by one, but many, often tens of thousands, in a single day. And death is no longer a chance event. To be sure, it still seems a matter of chance whether a bullet hits this man or that; but a second bullet may well hit the survivor; and the accumulation of deaths puts an end to the impression of chance. Life has, indeed, become interesting again; it has recovered its full content.

Here a distinction should be made between two groups—those who themselves risk their lives in battle, and those who have stayed at home and have only to wait for the loss of one of their dear ones by wounds, disease, or infection. It would be most interesting, no doubt, to study the changes in the psychology of the combatants, but I know too little about it. We must restrict ourselves to the second group, to which we ourselves belong. I have said already that in my opinion the bewilderment and the paralysis of capacity, from which we suffer, are essentially determined among other things by the circumstance that we are unable to maintain our former attitude towards death, and have not yet found a new one. It may assist us to do this if we direct our psychological enquiry towards two other relations to death—the one which we may ascribe to primaeval, prehistoric men, and the one which still exists in every one of us, but which conceals itself, invisible to consciousness, in the deeper strata of our mental life.

What the attitude of prehistoric man was towards death is, of course, only known to us by inferences and constructions, but I believe that these methods have furnished us with fairly trustworthy conclusions.

Primaeval man took up a very remarkable attitude towards death. It was far from consistent; it was indeed most contradictory. On the one hand, he took death seriously, recognized it as the termination of life and made use of it in that sense; on the other hand, he also denied death and reduced it to nothing. This contradiction arose from the fact that he took up radically different attitudes towards the death of other people, of strangers, of enemies, and towards his own. He had no objection to someone else's death; it meant the annihilation of someone he hated, and primitive man had no scruples against bringing it about. He was no doubt a very passionate creature and more cruel and more malignant than other animals. He liked to kill, and killed as a matter of course. The instinct which is said to restrain other animals from killing and devouring their own species need not be attributed to him.

Hence the primaeval history of mankind is filled with murder. Even today, the history of the world which our children learn at school is essentially a series of murders of peoples. The obscure sense of guilt to which mankind has been subject since prehistoric times, and which in some religions has been condensed into the doctrine of primal guilt, of original sin, is probably the outcome of a blood-guilt incurred by prehistoric man. In my *book Totem and Taboo* (1912–13) I have, following clues given by Robertson Smith, Atkinson, and Charles Darwin, tried to guess the nature of this primal guilt, and I believe, too, that the Christian doctrine of today enables us to deduce it. If the Son of God was obliged to sacrifice his life to redeem mankind from original sin, then by the law of talion, the requital of like by like, that sin must have been a killing, a murder. Nothing else could call for the sacrifice of a life for its expiation. And the original sin was an offence against God the Father, the primal crime of mankind must have been a parricide, the killing of the primal father of the primitive human horde, whose mnemic image was later transfigured into a deity.

His own death was certainly just as unimaginable and unreal for primaeval man as it is for any one of us today. But there was for him one case in which the two opposite attitudes towards death collided and came into conflict with each other; and this case became highly important and productive of far-reaching consequences. It occurred when primaeval man saw someone who belonged to him die—his wife, his child, his friend—whom he undoubtedly loved as we love ours, for love cannot be much younger than the lust to kill. Then, in his pain, he was forced to learn that one can die, too, oneself, and his whole being revolted against the admission; for each of these loved ones was, after all, a part of his own beloved self. But, on the other hand, deaths such as these pleased him as well, since in each of the loved persons there was also something of the stranger. The law of ambivalence of feeling, which to this day governs our emotional relations with those whom we love most, certainly had a very much wider validity in primaeval times. Thus these beloved dead had also been enemies and strangers who had aroused in him some degree of hostile feeling.

Philosophers have declared that the intellectual enigma presented to primaeval man by the picture of death forced him to reflection, and thus became the starting-point of all speculation. I believe that here the philosophers are thinking too philosophically, and giving too little consideration to the motives that were primarily operative. I should like therefore to limit and correct their assertion. In my view, primaeval man must have triumphed beside the body of his slain enemy, without being led to rack his brains about the enigma of life and death. What released the spirit of enquiry in man was not the intellectual enigma, and not every death, but the conflict of feeling at the death of loved yet alien and hated persons. Of this conflict of feeling psychology was the first offspring. Man could no longer keep death at a distance, for he had tasted it in his pain about the dead; but he was nevertheless unwilling to acknowledge it, for he could not conceive of himself as dead. So he devised a compromise:

he conceded the fact of his own death as well, but denied it the significance of annihilation—a significance which he had had no motive for denying where the death of his enemy was concerned. It was beside the dead body of someone he loved that he invented spirits, and his sense of guilt at the satisfaction mingled with his sorrow turned these new-born spirits into evil demons that had to be dreaded. The [physical] changes brought about by death suggested to him the division of the individual into a body and a soul—originally several souls. In this way his train of thought ran parallel with the process of disintegration which sets in with death. His persisting memory of the dead became the basis for assuming other forms of existence and gave him the conception of a life continuing after apparent death.

These subsequent existences were at first no more than appendages to the existence which death had brought to a close—shadowy, empty of content, and valued at little until later times; they still bore the character of wretched makeshifts. We may recall the answer made to Odysseus by the soul of Achilles:

> For of old, when thou wast alive, we Argives honoured thee even as the gods, and now that thou art here, thou rulest mightily over the dead. Wherefore grieve not at all that thou art dead, Achilles.
>
> So I spoke, and he straightway made answer and said: "Nay, seek not to speak soothingly to me of death, glorious Odysseus. I should choose, so I might live on earth, to serve as the hireling of another, of some portionless man whose livelihood was but small, rather than to be lord over all the dead that have perished."

Or in Heine's powerful and bitter parody:

Der kleinste lebendige Philister
Zu Stuckert am Neckar
Viel glücklicher ist er
Als ich, der Pelide, der tote Held,
Der Schattenfürst in der Unterwelt.[1]

It was only later that religions succeeded in representing this after-life as the more desirable, the truly valid one, and in reducing the life which is ended by death to a mere preparation. After this, it was no more than consistent to extend life backwards into the past, to form the notion of earlier existences, of the transmigration of souls and of reincarnation, all with the purpose of depriving death of its meaning as the termination of life. So early did the denial of death, which we have described as a "conventional and cultural attitude," have its origin.

What came into existence beside the dead body of the loved one was not only the doctrine of the soul, the belief in immortality and a powerful source of man's sense of guilt, but also the earliest ethical commandments. The first and most important prohibition made by the awakening conscience was: "Thou shalt not kill." It was acquired in relation to dead people who were loved, as a reaction against the satisfaction of the hatred hidden behind the grief for them; and it was gradually extended to strangers who were not loved,

---

1   [From the German: "The smallest living philistine in the town of Stuckert-am-Neckar is far happier than I, Pelides (Achilles), the dead hero, the shadow-prince in the underworld." The closing lines of "Departure," one of the very last of Heinrich Heine's poems.]

and finally even to enemies.

This final extension of the commandment is no longer experienced by civilized man. When the furious struggle of the present war has been decided, each one of the victorious fighters will return home joyfully to his wife and children, unchecked and undisturbed by thoughts of the enemies he has killed whether at close quarters or at long range. It is worthy of note that the primitive races which still survive in the world, and are undoubtedly closer than we are to primaeval man, act differently in this respect, or did until they came under the influence of our civilization. Savages—Australians, Bushmen, Tierra del Fuegans—are far from being remorseless murderers; when they return victorious from the war-path they may not set foot in their villages or touch their wives till they have atoned for the murders they committed in war by penances which are often long and tedious. It is easy, of course, to attribute this to their superstition: the savage still goes in fear of the avenging spirits of the slain. But the spirits of his slain enemy are nothing but the expression of his bad conscience about his blood-guilt; behind this superstition there lies concealed a vein of ethical sensitiveness which has been lost by us civilized men.

Pious souls, no doubt, who would like to believe that our nature is remote from any contact with what is evil and base, will not fail to use the early appearance and the urgency of the prohibition against murder as the basis for gratifying conclusions as to the strength of the ethical impulses which must have been implanted in us. Unfortunately this argument proves even more for the opposite view. So powerful a prohibition can only be directed against an equally powerful impulse. What no human soul desires stands in no need of prohibition; it is excluded automatically. The very emphasis laid on the commandment "Thou shalt not kill" makes it certain that we spring from an endless series of generations of murderers, who had the lust for killing in their blood, as, perhaps, we ourselves have today. Mankind's ethical strivings, whose strength and significance we need not in the least depreciate, were acquired in the course of man's history; since then they have become, though unfortunately only in a very variable amount, the inherited property of contemporary men.

Let us now leave primaeval man, and turn to the unconscious in our own mental life. Here we depend entirely upon the psycho-analytic method of investigation, the only one which reaches to such depths. What, we ask, is the attitude of our unconscious towards the problem of death? The answer must be: almost exactly the same as that of primaeval man. In this respect, as in many others, the man of prehistoric times survives unchanged in our unconscious. Our unconscious, then, does not believe in its own death; it behaves as if it were immortal. What we call our "unconscious"—the deepest strata of our minds, made up of instinctual impulses— knows nothing that is negative, and no negation; in it contradictories coincide. For that reason it does not know its own death, for to that we can give only a negative content. Thus there is nothing instinctual in us which responds to a belief in death. This may even be the secret of heroism. The rational grounds for heroism rest on a judgement that the subject's own life cannot be so precious as certain abstract and general goods. But more frequent, in my view, is the instinctive and impulsive heroism which knows no such reasons, and flouts danger in the spirit of Anzengruber's *Steinklopferhans:* "Nothing can happen to me." Or else those reasons only serve to clear away the hesitations which might old back the heroic reaction that corresponds to the unconscious. The fear of death, which dominates us oftener than we know, is on the other hand something secondary, and is usually the outcome of a sense of guilt.

On the other hand, for strangers and for enemies we do acknowledge death, and consign them to it quite as readily and unhesitatingly as did primaeval man. There is, it is true, a distinction here which will be pronounced decisive so far as real life is concerned. Our unconscious does not carry out the killing; It merely thinks it and wishes it. But it would be wrong so completely to undervalue this psychical reality as compared with factual reality. It is significant and momentous enough. In our unconscious impulses we daily and hourly get rid of anyone who stands in our way, of anyone who has offended or injured us. The expression "Devil take him!", which so often comes to people's lips in joking anger and which really means "Death take him!", is in our unconscious a serious and powerful death-wish. Indeed, our unconscious will murder even for trifles; like the ancient Athenian code of Draco, it knows no other punishment for crime than death. And this has a certain consistency, for every injury to our almighty and autocratic ego is at bottom a crime of *lèse-majesté.*

And so, if we are to be judged by our unconscious wishful impulses, we ourselves are, like primaeval man, a gang of murderers. It is fortunate that all these wishes do not possess the potency that was attributed to them in primaeval times; in the cross-fire of mutual curses mankind would long since have perished, the best and wisest of men and the loveliest and fairest of women with the rest.

Psycho-analysis finds as a rule no credence among laymen for assertions such as these. They reject them as calumnies which are confuted by conscious experience, and they adroitly overlook the faint indications by which even the unconscious is apt to betray itself to consciousness. It is therefore relevant to point out that many thinkers who could not have been influenced by psycho-analysis have quite definitely accused our unspoken thoughts of being ready, heedless of the prohibition against murder, to get rid of anything which stands in our way. From many examples of this I will choose one that has become famous:

In *Le Père Goriot,* Balzac alludes to a passage in the works of J. J. Rousseau where that author asks the reader what he would do if—without leaving Paris and of course without being discovered—he could kill, with great profit to himself, an old mandarin in Peking by a mere act of will. Rousseau implies that he would not give much for the life of that dignitary. "*Tuer son mandarin*" has become a proverbial phrase for this secret readiness, present even in modern man.

There are also a whole number of cynical jokes and anecdotes which reveal the same tendency—such, for instance, as the words attributed to a husband: "If one of us two dies, I shall move to Paris." Such cynical jokes would not be possible unless they contained an unacknowledged truth which could not be admitted if it were expressed seriously and without disguise. In jest—it is well known—one may even tell the truth.

Just as for primaeval man, so also for our unconscious, there is one case in which the two opposing attitudes

towards death, the one which acknowledges it as the annihilation of life and the other which denies it as unreal, collide
and come into conflict. This case is the same as in primal
ages: the death, or the risk of death, of someone we love, a
parent or a partner in marriage, a brother or sister, a child
or a dear friend. These loved ones are on the one hand an
inner possession, components of our own ego; but on the
other hand they are partly strangers, even enemies. With
the exception of only a very few situations, there adheres
to the tenderest and most intimate of our love-relations a
small portion of hostility which can excite an unconscious
death-wish. But this conflict due to ambivalence does not
now, as it did then, lead to the doctrine of the soul and to
ethics, but to neurosis, which affords us deep insight into
normal mental life as well. How often have physicians who
practise psycho-analysis had to deal with the symptom of
an exaggerated worry over the well-being of relatives, or
with entirely unfounded self-reproaches after the death of a
loved person. The study of such phenomena has left them in
no doubt about the extent and importance of unconscious
death-wishes.

The layman feels an extraordinary horror at the possibility of such feelings, and takes this aversion as a legitimate
ground for disbelief in the assertions of psycho-analysis.
Mistakenly, I think. No depreciation of feelings of love is
intended, and there is in fact none. It is indeed foreign to
our intelligence as well as to our feelings thus to couple love
and hate; but Nature, by making use of this pair of opposites,
contrives to keep love ever vigilant and fresh, so as to guard
it against the hate which lurks behind it. It might be said
that we owe the fairest flowerings of our love to the reaction

against the hostile impulse which we sense within us.

To sum up: our unconscious is just as inaccessible to the idea of our own death, just as murderously inclined towards strangers, just as divided (that is, ambivalent) towards those we love, as was primaeval man. But how far we have moved from this primal state in our conventional and cultural attitude towards death!

It is easy to see how war impinges on this dichotomy. It strips us of the later accretions of civilization, and lays bare the primal man in each of us. It compels us once more to be heroes who cannot believe in their own death; it stamps strangers as enemies, whose death is to be brought about or desired; it tells us to disregard the death of those we love. But war cannot be abolished; so long as the conditions of existence among nations are so different and their mutual repulsion so violent, there are bound to be wars. The question then arises: Is it not we who should give in, who should adapt ourselves to war? Should we not confess that in our civilized attitude towards death we are once again living psychologically beyond our means, and should we not rather turn back and recognize the truth? Would it not be better to give death the place in reality and in our thoughts, which is its due, and to give a little more prominence to the unconscious attitude towards death which we have hitherto so carefully suppressed? This hardly seems an advance to higher achievement, but rather in some respects a backward step—a regression; but it has the advantage of taking the truth more into account, and of making life more tolerable for us once again. To tolerate life remains, after all, the first duty of all living beings. Illusion becomes valueless if it makes this harder for us.

We recall the old saying: *Si vis pacem, para bellum.* If you want to preserve peace, arm for war.

It would be in keeping with the times to alter it: *Si vis vitam, para mortem.* If you want to endure life, prepare yourself for death.

ALBERT EINSTEIN ON PEACE

THE 1932 DISARMAMENT CONFERENCE[1]

The fruits of man's inventive genius over the past century might well have made life carefree and happy, had our institutions been able to keep up with the advance of technology. As it is, these hard-won achievements are, in the hands of our generation, as dangerous as a gun wielded by a toddler. Possession of our wonderful means of production has generated want and famine, and not freedom.

Technological progress is most pernicious when it serves to destroy human life and the hard-won products of human labor, as we of the older generation witnessed to our horror in the World War. But more terrible even than this kind of destruction is, to my mind, the abject servitude which war forces upon the individual. What could be worse than to be compelled, by society, into actions which all of us as individuals regard as heinous crimes! And how few had the moral courage to resist. In my eyes they are the true heroes of the World War.

There is, however, one ray of hope. It seems to me that the responsible leaders of the nations today do, in the main, sincerely wish to abolish war. Resistance to this absolutely necessary measure centers in the unfortunate traditions of

1   To *The Nation,* New York, writing from Berlin on September 4; published September 23, 1931, on the upcoming Geneva armaments conference.

the various nations. These traditions are passed on, through the machinery of the educational system, like a hereditary disease from generation to generation. The principal villains in perpetuating these traditions are military training, its glorification and, equally, that sector of the press which is controlled by heavy industry and the military. Without disarmament there can be no enduring peace. Conversely, continuation of the arms race at the present pace will inexorably lead to new disasters.

That is why the Disarmament Conference of 1932 will be of crucial importance to this generation and the next. When one considers how pitiable, on the whole, have been the results of past conferences, it becomes obvious that all thoughtful and responsible people must do all they can to alert the public to the tremendous importance of this conference. Only if the statesmen have powerful support for a policy of peace from a majority of their people can they hope to attain their great goals. To help shape public opinion in that direction by words and deeds is the responsibility of all of us.

The doom of the conference would be sealed if the delegates arrived with rigid policy instructions, the realization of which would at once become a matter of national prestige. This danger, it seems, is being recognized on all sides. During the recent series of bilateral conferences, statesmen have endeavored to prepare the ground for the Disarmament Conference. This seems to me a very promising device; two men or two groups of men can usually thrash out their differences more reasonably, honestly and dispassionately when no third party is listening in, in the presence of whom they must be careful about what they say.

Only if the conference is being prepared in this painstaking manner, if surprise maneuvers are thus ruled out and if an atmosphere of confidence is created through genuine good will, can we hope for a successful result.

In such affairs of state success is not a matter of brilliance, still less of shrewdness; rather, it is a question of sincerity and trust. Sheer intelligence, thank heaven, cannot be a substitute for moral integrity.

The individual observer cannot afford merely to wait and criticize. He must serve the cause as best he can. The world's fate will be the one it deserves.

THE DANGER TO CIVILIZATION[1]

I MUST NOW PERMIT myself to turn to a second subject, which cannot be left unmentioned today, if a man does not wish to incur the suspicion of intentional silence. The basis of our European-American civilization is critically shaken, and a feeling of perplexity and fear has mastered all in the face of the immediate internal forces that threaten us in our existence. At a time when we are rich in consumable goods and means of production as no previous generation before us, a great part of humanity suffers severe want; production and consumption falter to an increasing degree; and confidence in public institutions has sunk as never before. It is as if the circulatory system of the whole economic organism were throughout, fatally ill.

Much indeed has been philosophized as to the origin of this illness, and it appears as if purely technical remedies might produce a cure. "Why should the equilibrium between production and consumption not let itself be re-established by suitable measures?" So asks the optimist. But the pessimist asks: "Why should not our civilization collapse through inner decay, in a manner similar to that of the Roman empire?" Who is right? Where do we stand?

I will try to answer, with the help of a look into the past.

1   Excerpt of a speech given at a dinner in Einstein's honor by the California Institute of Technology, Pasadena, January 25, 1932.

Our material civilization has as its permanent justification the protection and development of our culture. This, however, receives its sustenance from two springs. The first derives from the Hellenistic spirit and experienced its renewal and completion in the Italian Renaissance. It encounters the individual with the command: "Think, observe, and create." The second comes from the Hebraic and early Christian. It is characterized by the maxim: "Save thy soul by unselfish service to common humanity." We can in this way speak of a creative and of an ethical spring for our culture. Until nearly the end of the Middle Ages the vitality of our culture was fed only from the second spring; this culture was miserable but stable. Then at the time of the Renaissance when the creative spring began to flow more exuberantly, there began an ever-growing flowering of culture, which has lasted until our own day, and with which each successive generation has become intoxicated. A powerful civilization and technique, combined with an unsuspected increase in population, and a rise in the physical and intellectual standards of life, was the result of this feverish development.

We had so to say forgotten, that the ethical spring is also a necessary condition for our being. Now, however, in the time of sickness, we must see with alarm, that this spring has critically retreated; and without it we are irretrievably exposed to disaster. The more powerful are the tools which the creative force of past generations has given into our hand, just so much greater and purer must be the ethical forces that are necessary to make a wholesome use thereof. It is not in intelligence that we lack for the overcoming of evil, but we lack in the unselfish responsible devotion of men in the service of the common weal.

Must I prove this in detail? Do we not experience every day in nearly all countries that the sense of justice in the people is not sufficient to bring about the reversal of legal judgements, which are regarded by the people as false judgements? Do we not cling to international agreements, whose economic impossibility has long been known but not publicly recognized. Do not the nations undertake material and psychological preparations for warlike acts, when there is no doubt as to their disastrous results for mankind and their incompatibility with the officially recognized ethical principles? Each can continue such questions further without end; but he receives as his only answer a sceptical smile. Heinrich Heine, however, sang with bitterness: "And a fool waits for his answer."

I conclude with a thankful recognition of the free and hospitable institutions of this country, which make it possible to speak in this wide circle with openness.

Albert Einstein and Sigmund Freud:
A Meeting of Great Minds
by Ulrich Baer

ALBERT EINSTEIN, THE great scientist and discoverer of
relativity, and Sigmund Freud, the founder of the theory
and practice of psychoanalysis, met only once in person, in
Berlin in 1927 during the New Year's Eve festivities. They
enjoyed each other's company, although Einstein declined
the invitation to be psychoanalyzed by commenting: "I prefer
to remain in the darkness of my state of not being analyzed."
Freud wrote after their meeting: "[Einstein] is cheerful, con-
fident, and charming, understands psychology as much as I
understand physics, and in this way we had a very pleasant
conversation." Einstein praised Freud as the greatest writer
since philosopher Arthur Schopenhauer. While Freud
appreciated the compliment, he noted in another letter that
Einstein lauded his style because he lacked an understanding of the content of Freud's writings. Today we know that
while Einstein greatly admired and personally liked Freud,
he also declined to support an effort to have Freud considered for the Nobel Prize, given Einstein's uncertainty about
the scientific tenability of Freud's theories.

In 1932, Einstein was asked by the International Institute
of Intellectual Cooperation of the League of Nations

(founded in Geneva in 1920 to provide a forum for resolving international disputes by peaceful means) to invite a public figure to comment on a topic of general concern. By that time, the scientist had become widely known as a political commentator and committed pacifist. Einstein selected Freud to respond to his open letter addressing the persistence of war in the modern age in the hope of outlining some ways to prevent it. Freud had also published several important books on culture, religion, and human concerns in general, in addition to his enormously influential psychoanalytic writings. In his letter of invitation, Einstein stressed the importance of establishing an independent, international judiciary body to mediate conflicts. He also noted the difficulty of enforcing any rules created by such a body without an independent armed force. Freud agreed with this idea but also cautioned that "there is no likelihood of our being able to suppress humanity's aggressive tendencies." Only in his concluding sentence did Freud permit himself to suggest that "whatever makes for cultural development is working also against war," which differs somewhat from more pessimistic positions he takes elsewhere in his writings. In a conversation with an official from the League of Nations who facilitated the exchange, Freud warned that his letter would also contain several unwelcome truths about the persistence of man's innate aggressive tendencies.

Drawing on theories he developed earlier and especially in his 1930 publication *Civilization and Its Discontents*, Freud proposed that war is rooted in an innate drive for destruction and perhaps among the inevitable expressions of man's distaste for the restraints of civilization. Einstein considered himself a "militant pacifist." Throughout the course of his illustrious career he gave many speeches and published numerous statements and open letters against the cult of militarism, in support of conscientious objectors, and against armament. In his letter and anticipated some of Freud's insights.

The exchange was simultaneously published in German, English, and French in 1933. By that time Hitler had risen to power in Germany and the threat of war was growing more ominous with each passing month. Einstein had left his native Germany in 1932, renounced his German citizenship, and moved in October of 1933 to the United States, where he became a citizen in 1940. Freud remained in Vienna, where he had spent his adult life, until emigrating to London in 1938, following the German annexation of Austria.

The correspondence between Einstein and Freud remains dismayingly relevant to this day. Their letters brought together the perspectives of one of the greatest scientists of all time and the groundbreaking founder of psychoanalysis—each of them responsible for radically transforming their respective disciplines. Their exchange offers a unique interdisciplinary exploration of some of the destructive challenges facing humanity and constitutes a rare collaboration of two unparalleled thinkers who devoted themselves to understanding our existence on both a universal and a human scale.

Also from Warbler Press

More original and classic titles at warblerpress.com